Colour
Therapy

Really Relaxing Colouring Book 10

First published in 2015 by Kyle Craig Publishing

Text and illustration copyright © 2015 Kyle Craig Publishing

Editor: Alison McNicol

Design: Julie Anson

ISBN: 978-1-908707-95-6

A CIP record for this book is available from the British Library.

A Kyle Craig Publication

www.kyle-craig.com